WITHDRAWN

The 1971 Pere Marquette
Theology Lecture

DOCTRINAL PLURALISM

by

BERNARD LONERGAN, S.J.

Marquette University Press
Milwaukee 1971

Library of Congress Catalog Number 70-155364

ISBN 0-87462-503-3

Second Printing, 1972

Third Printing, 1978

PRINTED
IN
U. S. A.

Prefatory

In conjunction with the Tercentenary celebration of the missions and explorations of Jacques Marquette, S.J., the university's namesake, the Marquette University Theology Department launched a series of annual public lectures by distinguished theologians under the title of "The Pere Marquette Theology Lectures."

The 1971 lecture was delivered in Uihlein Hall of Milwaukee's new Performing Arts Center on the afternoon of Saturday, April 3rd, by the Rev. Bernard Lonergan, S.J., S.T.D., professor of dogmatic theology at Regis College, Toronto.

Bernard Lonergan was born in Buckingham, Quebec, on December 17, 1904. He earned the B.A. at the University of London in 1930, the S.T.D. at the Gregorian University, Rome, in 1940. He has taught theology at L'Immaculée Conception (Montreal), at the Jesuit Seminary (Toronto), and at the Gregorian University. Next year he will be at Harvard.

In 1947 Father Lonergan received the Cardinal Spellman Award for outstanding theological scholarship. In 1970 his work was the subject of "The First International Lonergan Congress." In the same year the Canadian government paid him its highest honor, naming him a Companion of the Order of Canada.

His published writings include: *Insight: A Study of Human Understanding* (London, New York, Longmans, Green, 1957); *Collection* (New York, Herder and Herder, 1967); *Verbum, Word and Idea in Aquinas* (Notre Dame, Notre Dame University Press, 1967); *The Subject* (Marquette University Press, 1968); and articles in many philosophical and theological journals.

Father Lonergan has appeared at Marquette many times in recent years. He delivered "Dimensions of Meaning" here in 1965 and "The Subject" in 1968. In 1970 Marquette awarded him the degree of Doctor of Letters, *honoris causa.*

Doctrinal Pluralism

A discussion of a pluralism in church doctrines needs a rather broad context. Accordingly my remarks will come under the following series of headings:

1. Pluralism and Communications
2. Pluralism and Classicist Culture
3. Pluralism and Relativism
4. Undifferentiated and Differentiated Consciousness
5. Pluralism and Theological Doctrines
6. Pluralism and Conversion
7. Pluralism and Church Doctrines: The First Vatican Council
8. Pluralism and Church Doctrines: The Ongoing Context
9. The Permanence and Historicity of Dogma
10. Pluralism and the Unity of Faith
11. The Permanence of Dogma and Demythologization

1. *Pluralism and Communications*

In the final paragraph of the gospel according to Matthew, our Lord bid the

Eleven to go forth and make all nations his
disciples. This command has always stood
at the basis of the church's mission, but in
our age it has taken on a special signifi-
cance. On the one hand, anthropological
and historical research has made us aware
of the enormous variety of human mentali-
ties, cultures, and social arrangements. On
the other hand, even a brief experience of
historical investigation makes one aware
how diligently yet how circumspectly one
must proceed if one is to hope to recon-
struct the meanings and intentions of another people, another time, another place.
So it is that now we can know so much
more about all nations and about the differences among them. So too it is that now
we can understand the vastness and the
complexity of the task of preaching the
gospel to all nations.

This fact of diversity entails a pluralism, not yet of doctrines, but at least of
communications. If one doctrine is to be
preached to all, still it is not to be preached
in the same manner to all.[1] If one is to
communicate with those of another cul-

ture, one must employ the resources of
their culture. To employ simply the re-
source's of one's own culture is not to communicate with the other but to remain
locked up in one's own. On the other hand,
it is not enough simply to employ the resources of the other culture; one must do
so creatively. Merely to employ the resources of the other culture would be to
fail to communicate the Christian mes-
sage. But creative employment of those
resources makes it possible to say in that
culture what as yet had not been said.

There is a further point. Once Christian doctrine has been introduced successfully within a culture, it will proceed to
develop along the lines of that culture. So
it was that the gospel first preached in
Palestine developed into a Judaic Christianity that employed the thought-forms
and stylistic genera of *Spätjudentum* in its
apprehension of the Christian mysteries.[2]
So too down the ages there have developed the idiosyncrasies of many local or
national churches. Nor do these ongoing
differences, once they are understood and

explained, threaten the unity of faith.
Rather they testify to its vitality. For, as
once was said, *quidquid recipitur ad mo-
dum recipientis recipitur,* while the absence of varying modalities would seem
to prove an absence of genuine assimilation and the presence of only a perfunc-
tory acceptance.

2. *Pluralism and Classicist Culture*

The contemporary notion of culture is
empirical. A culture is a set of meanings
and values informing a common way of
life, and there are as many cultures as
there are distinct sets of such meanings
and values.

But this manner of conceiving culture
is relatively recent. It is a product of empirical human studies. Within less than
one hundred years it has replaced an older
classicist view that had flourished for over
two millenia. On the older view culture
was conceived normatively. It was the op-
posite of barbarism. It was a matter of
acquiring and assimilating the tastes and
skills, the ideals, virtues and ideas that
were pressed upon one in a good home

and through a curriculum in the liberal
arts. It stressed not facts but values. It
could not but claim to be universalist. Its
classics were immortal works of art, its
philosophy was the perennial philosophy,
its laws and structures were the deposit of
the prudence and the wisdom of mankind.
Classicist education was a matter of models
to be imitated, of ideal characters to be
emulated, of eternal verities and univer-
sally valid laws. It sought to produce not
the mere specialist but the *uomo univer-
sale* that could turn his hand to anything
and do it brilliantly.

The classicist is not a pluralist. He
knows that circumstances alter cases but
he is far more deeply convinced that circumstances are accidental and that, beyond them, there is some substance or
kernel or root that fits in the classicist assumptions of stability, immutability, fixity.
Things have their specific natures; these
natures, at least in principle, are to be
known exhaustively through the properties
they possess and the laws they obey; and
over and above the specific nature there

is only individuation by matter, so that knowledge of one instance of a species automatically is knowledge of any instance. What is true of species in general, also is true of the human species, of the one faith coming through Jesus Christ, of the one charity given through the gift of the Holy Spirit. It follows that the diversities of peoples, cultures, social arrangements can involve only a difference in the dress in which church doctrine is expressed, but cannot involve any diversity in church doctrine itself. That is *semper idem.*

The pluralist begs to differ. He insists that human concepts are products and expressions of human understanding, that human understanding develops over time, and that it develops differently in different places and in different times. Again, he would claim that a human action, determined solely by abstract properties, abstract principles, abstract laws, would be not only abstract but also inhumanly inept on every concrete occasion. For possible courses of human action are the discoveries of human intelligence, perhaps remotely guided by principles and laws, but certainly grasped by insight into concrete situations. Moreover, it is by further insight that the probable results of each possible course of action are determined, and that determination, so far from settling the issue, stands in need of a free and hopefully responsible choice before action can ensue. Finally, in so far as a situation or a course of action is intelligible, it can recur; but the less intelligent people are, the less they learn from the defects of previous acts, and the more likely they are to settle into some routine that keeps repeating the same mistakes to make their situation ever worse. On the other hand, the more intelligent they are, the more they can learn from previous mistakes, and the more they will keep changing their situation and so necessitating still further changes in their courses of action.

The pluralist, then, differs from the classicist inasmuch as he acknowledges human historicity both in principle and in fact. Historicity means—very briefly—that human living is informed by meanings, that meanings are the product of intelligence, that human intelligence develops cumulatively over time, and that such cumulative development differs in different histories.

Classicism itself is one very notable and, indeed, very noble instance of such cumulative development. It is not mistaken in its assumption that there is something substantial and common to human nature and human activity. Its oversight is its failure to grasp that that something substantial and common also is something quite open. It may be expressed in the four transcendental precepts: Be attentive, Be intelligent, Be reasonable, Be responsible. But there is an almost endless manifold of situations to which men successively attend. There vary enormously the type and degree of intellectual and moral development brought to deal with situations. The standard both for human reasonableness and for the strength and delicacy of a man's conscience is satisfied only by a complete and life-long devotion to human authenticity.

I have been outlining the theoretic objections to classicist thought. Far more
massive are the factual objections. For a
century and a half there have been developing highly refined methods in hermeneutics and history, and there have been
multiplying not only new modes of study-
ing scripture, the Fathers, the Scholastics,
the Renaissance and Reformation, and
subsequent periods, but also there have
emerged numerous historically-minded
philosophies. To confine the Catholic
Church to a classicist mentality is to keep
the Catholic Church out of the modern
world and to prolong the already too long
prolonged crisis within the Church.

3. *Pluralism and Relativism*

As the breakdown of Scholasticism has
left many Catholics without any philosophy, so the rejection of the classicist outlook leaves many without even a *Weltan-
schauung*. In this state of almost complete
disorientation they feel confronted with
an endless relativism when they are told
that no one in this life can aspire to a
knowledge of all mathematics, or all

physics, or all chemistry, or all biology, or the whole of human studies, or of all the philosophies, or even of the whole of theology.

What is worse is that usually they are not equipped to deal effectively and successfully with the premisses set forth by relativists. These premisses are: (1) The meaning of any statement is relative to its context; (2) every context is subject to change; it stands within a process of development and/or decay; and (3) it is not possible to predict what the future context will be.

The trouble is twofold. On the one hand, these premisses, as far as they go, are true. On the other hand, the complement they need does not consist primarily in further propositions; it is to be found only by unveiling the invariant structure of man's conscious and intentional acts; and that unveiling is a long and difficult task.[3] That task cannot be even outlined here, and so we have to be content to indicate briefly the type of qualification that can and should be added to the premises of relativism.

It is true that the meaning of any statement is relative to its context. But it does not follow that the context is unknown or, if it is unknown, that it cannot be discovered.[4] Still less does it follow that the statement understood within its context is mistaken or false. On the contrary, there are many true statements whose context is easily ascertained.

It is true that contexts change, and it can happen that a statement, which was true in its own context, ceases to be adequate in another context. It remains that it was true in its original context, that sound historical and exegetical procedures can reconstitute the original context with greater or less success and, in the same measure, arrive at an apprehension of the original truth.

It is true that one cannot predict in detail what future changes of context will occur. But one can predict, for example, that the contexts of descriptive statements are less subject to change than the contexts of explanatory statements. Again, with regard to explanatory statements, one can predict that a theory that radically revised the periodic table of chemical elements would account not only for all the data accounted for by the periodic table but also for a substantial range of data for which the periodic table does not account.

Finally, as already remarked, if one wishes a more solid and searching treatment of the issue, one has to undertake a thorough exploration of the three basic issues in philosophy, namely, what am I doing when I am knowing (cognitional theory), why is doing that knowing (epistemology), and what do I know when I do it (metaphysics).

4.   *Undifferentiated and Variously Differentiated Consciousness*

For centuries theologians were divided into schools. The schools differed from one another on most points in systematic theology. But they all shared a common origin in medieval Scholasticism and so they were able to understand one another and could attempt, if not dialogue, at least refutation. But with the breakdown of Scholasticism that common ancestry is no longer a bond. The widest divergences in doctrine are being expressed by Catholic theologians. If each abounds in his wisdom, he also tends to be mystified by the existence of views other than his own.

If one is to understand this enormous diversity, one must, I believe, advert to the sundry differentiations of human consciousness. A first differentiation arises in the process of growing up. The infant lives in a world of immediacy. The child moves towards a world mediated by meaning. For the adult the real world is the world mediated by meaning, and his philosophic doubts about the reality of that world arise from the fact that he has failed to advert to the difference between the criteria for a world of immediacy and, on the other hand, the criteria for the world mediated by meaning.

Such inadvertence seems to be the root of the confusion concerning objects and objectivity that has obtained in Western

thought since Kant published his *Critique
of Pure Reason.*[5] In the world of immediacy the only objects are objects of experience, where "experience" is understood in the narrow sense and denotes
either the outer experience of sense or the
inner experience of consciousness. But in
the world mediated by meaning — i.e.,
mediated by experiencing, understanding,
and judging—objects are what are intended by questions and known by intelligent,
correct, conscientious answers. It is by his
questions for intelligence *(quid sit, cur ita
sit),* for reflection *(an sit),* for moral de-
liberation *(an honestum sit),* that man in-
tends without yet knowing the intelligible,
the true, the real, and the good. By that
intending man is immediately related to
the objects that he will come to know
when he elicits correct acts of meaning.
Accordingly, naive realism arises from the
assumption that the world mediated by
meaning is known by taking a look. Em-
piricism arises when the world mediated
by meaning is emptied of everything except what can be seen, heard, felt. Ideal-

ism retains the empiricist notion of reality,
insists that human knowledge consists in
raising and answering questions, and con-
cludes that human knowledge is not of the
real but of the ideal. Finally, a critical
realism claims that adult human knowledge of reality consists not in experiencing alone but in experiencing, understanding, and judging.

Besides the differentiation of consciousness involved in growing up, further
differentiations occur with respect to the
world mediated by meaning. Here the
best known is the differentiation of commonsense meaning and scientific meaning.
Its origins are celebrated in Plato's
early dialogues in which Socrates explains
what he means by a definition that applies
omni et soli, seeks definitions of courage,
sobriety, justice, and the like, shows the
inadequacy of any proposed definition,
admits that he himself is unable to answer
his own questions. But a generation or so
later in Aristotle's *Nicomachean Ethics* we
find not only general definitions of virtue
and vice but also definitions of an array

of specific virtues each one flanked by vices that sin by excess or by defect. However, Aristotle not merely answered Socrates' questions but also set up the possibility of answering them by a sustained scrutiny of linguistic usage, by selecting the precise meaning he assigned to the terms he employed, by constructing sets of interrelated terms, and by employing such sets to systematize whole regions of inquiry.

Thereby was effected the differentiation of commonsense meaning and scientific meaning. Socrates and his friends knew perfectly well what they meant by courage, sobriety, justice. But such knowledge does not consist in universal definitions. It consists simply in understanding when the term may be used appropriately, and such understanding is developed by adverting to the response others give to one's statements. As it does not define, so too common sense does not enounce universal principles; it offers proverbs, i.e., pieces of advice it may be well to bear in mind when the occasion arises; hence

"Strike the iron while it is hot" and "He
who hesitates is lost" are not so much con-
tradicted as complemented by "Look before you leap." Finally, common sense
does not syllogize; it argues from analogy;
but its analogies resemble, not those con-
structed by logicians, in which the ana-
logue partly is similar and partly dis-
similar, but rather Piaget's adaptations
which consist in two parts: an assimilation
that calls on the insights relevant to some-
what similar situations; and an adjustment
that adds insights relevant to the pecu-
liarities of the present situation.

But besides the world mediated by
commonsense meanings, there is another
world mediated by scientific meanings,
where terms are defined, systematic rela-
tionships are sought, procedures are gov-
erned by logics and methods. This second
world was intuited by Plato's distinction
between the flux of phenomena and the
immutable Forms. It was affirmed more
soberly in Aristotle's distinction between
the *priora quoad nos* and the *priora quoad
se*. It has reappeared in Eddington's two

tables: one brown, solid, heavy; the other colorless, mostly empty space, with here and there an unimaginable wavicle. So it is that scientists live in two worlds: at one moment they are with the rest of us in the world of common sense; at another they are apart from us and by themselves with a technical and controlled language of their own and with reflectively construct-ed and controlled cognitional procedures.

Besides the scientific there is a relig-ious differentiation of consciousness. It begins with asceticism and culminates in mysticism. Both asceticism and mysticism, when genuine, have a common ground. That ground was described by St. Paul when he exclaimed: ". . . God's love has flooded our inmost heart through the Holy Spirit he has given us" (Rom 5, 5). That ground can bear fruit in a consciousness that lives in a world mediated by mean-ing. But it can also set up a different type of consciousness by withdrawing one from the world mediated by meaning into a cloud of unknowing.[6] Then one is for God, belongs to him, gives oneself to him, not by using images, concepts, words, but in a silent, joyous, peaceful surrender to his initiative.

Ordinarily the scientific and the religious differentiation of consciousness occur in different individuals. But they can be found in the same individual as was the case with Thomas of Aquin. At the end of his life his prayer was so intense that it interfered with his theological activity. But earlier there could have been an intermittent religious differentiation of consciousness, while later still further development might have enabled him to combine prayer and theology as Theresa of Avila combined prayer and business.

Besides the scientific and the religious there is the scholarly differentiation of consciousness. It combines the common sense of one's own place and time with a detailed understanding of the common sense of another place and time. It is a specifically modern achievement and it results only from a lifetime of study.

Besides the scientific, the religious, and the scholarly, there is the modern philosophic differentiation. Ancient and medieval philosophers were principally concerned with objects. If they attained any differentiation, that did not differ from the scientific. But in modern philosophy there has been a sustained tendency to begin, not from the objects in the world mediated by meaning, but from the immediate data of consciousness. In a first phase, from Descartes to Kant, the primary focus of attention was cognitional activity. But after the transition provided by German idealism, there was a notable shift in emphasis. Schopenhauer wrote on *Die Welt als Wille und Vorstellung;* Kierkegaard took his stand on faith; Newman took his on conscience; Nietzsche extolled the will to power; Dilthey aimed at a *Lebensphilosophie;* Blondel at a philosophy of action; Scheler was abundant on feeling; and similar tendencies, reminiscent of Kant's emphasis on practical reason, have been maintained by the personalists and the existentialists.

We have distinguished four differentiations of consciousness, the scientific, the religious, the scholarly, and the modern philosophic. We have noted the possibility of one compound differentiation in which the scientific and the religious were combined in a single individual. But there are five other possibilities of twofold differentiation,[7] and there are four possibilities of threefold differentiation.[8] Further, there is one case of fourfold differentiation in which scientific, religious, scholarly, and philosophic differentiations are combined. Finally, there is also one case of undifferentiated consciousness which is at home only in the realm of common sense: it shares Heidegger's affection for the pre-Socratics, the linguistic analyst's insistence on ordinary as opposed to technical language, and the strident devotion to the bible of those that want no dogmas.

There are then, on this analysis, sixteen different types of consciousness and from them result sixteen different worlds mediated by meaning. Still, this division is highly schematic. Further differences arise when one considers the degree to which consciousness has developed, the measure in which differentiated consciousness is integrated, the obnubilation imposed upon a consciousness that is less differentiated than its place and time demand, and the frustration imposed upon a consciousness that has achieved a greater differentiation than most other people in its social circle.

5.   *Pluralism and Theological Doctrines*

We have been considering diverse differentiations of human consciousness. Our aim has been to gain an insight into contemporary theological pluralism. It is time for us to set about applying the distinctions that have been drawn.

In general, the more differentiated consciousness is quite beyond the horizon of the less or the differently differentiated consciousness. Inversely, the less differentiated consciousness can easily be understood by the more differentiated, in so far as the former is included in the latter.

Undifferentiated consciousness is the most common type. To this type will always belong the vast majority of the faithful. As a type it can be understood by

everyone. But it itself is only mystified by
the subtleties of scientifically differentiated consciousness, by the oracles of
religiously differentiated consciousness, by
the strangeness of scholarly differentiated
consciousness, by the profundities of the
modern philosophic differentiation. One
can preach to it and teach it only by using
its own language, its own procedures, its
own resources. These are not uniform.
There are as many brands of common
sense as there are languages, socio-cul-
tural differences, almost differences of
place and time. The stranger is strange
because he comes from another place.
Hence to preach the gospel to all men
calls for at least as many men as there are
different places and times, and it requires
each of them to get to know the people to
whom he is sent, their manners and style
and ways of thought and speech. There
follows a manifold pluralism. Primarily it
is a pluralism, not of doctrine, but of communications. But within the realm of undifferentiated consciousness there is no
communication of doctrine except through

the available rituals, narratives, titles,
parables, metaphors, modes of praise and
blame, command and prohibition, promise
and threat.

An exception to this last statement
must be noted. The educated classes in a
society, such as was the Hellenistic, norm-
ally are instances of undifferentiated consciousness. But their education had among
its sources works of genuine philosophers,
so that they could be familiar with logical
principles and take propositions as the
objects on which they reflected and
operated. In this fashion the meaning of
homoousion for Athanasius was con-
tained in a rule concerning propositions
about the Father and the Son: *eadem de
Filio quae de Patre dicuntur excepto Patris
nomine.*[9] Again, the meaning of the one
person and two natures, mentioned in the
second paragraph of the decree of Chal-
cedon, stands forth in the repeated affirmation of the first paragraph that it is one
and the same Son our Lord Jesus Christ
that is perfect in divinity and the same
perfect in humanity, truly God and the

same truly man, consubstantial with the
Father in his divinity and the same consubstantial with us in his humanity, born
of the Father before the ages in his divinity and these last days the same ... born
of the Virgin Mary in his humanity.[10] Now
the meaning of the first paragraph can be
communicated without any new technical
terms. However, logical reflection on the
first paragraph will give rise to questions.
Is the humanity the same as the divinity?
If not, how can the same be both God and
man? It is only after these questions have
arisen in the mind of the inquirer that it is
relevant to explain that a distinction can
be drawn between person and nature, that
divinity and humanity denote two natures,
that it is one and the same person that is
both God and man. Such logical clarification is within the meaning of the decree.
But if one goes on to raise the metaphysical questions, such as the reality of
the distinction between person and nature,
one not only moves beyond the questions
explicitly envisaged by the decree but also

beyond the horizon of undifferentiated consciousness.

Turning now to religiously differentiated consciousness, we observe that it can be content with the negations of an apophatic theology. For it is in love, and on its love there are not any reservations or conditions or qualifications. It is with one's whole heart and whole soul and all one's mind and all one's strength. By such love a person is orientated positively to what is transcendent in lovableness. Such a positive orientation and the consequent self-surrender, as long as they are operative, enable one to dispense with any intellectually apprehended object;[11] and when they cease to be operative, the memory of them enables one to be content with enumerations of what God is not.

It may be objected that *nihil amatum nisi praecognitum.* But while that is true of other human love, it does not seem to be true of the love with which God floods our inmost heart through the Holy Spirit given to us. That grace is the finding that grounds our seeking God through natural

reason[12] and through positive religion.
That grace is the touchstone by which we
judge whether it is really God that natural
reason reaches or positive religion preach-
es. That grace would be the grace sufficient for salvation that God offers all men,
that underpins what is good in all the religions of mankind, that explains how
those that never heard the gospel can be
saved. That grace is what enables the
simple faithful to pray to their heavenly
Father in secret even though their religious apprehensions are faulty. That grace
is what replaces doctrine as the *unum
necessarium* in religions generally. That
grace indicates the theological justifica-
tion of Catholic dialogue with Christians,
with non-Christians, and even with
atheists who may love God in their hearts
without knowing him with their heads.

However, what is true of religions
generally, is not true of the Christian religion. For it knows God not only through
the grace in its heart but also through the
revelation of God's love in Christ Jesus
and the witness to that revelation down

the ages through the church. Christian
love of God is not just a state of mind and
heart; essential to it is the intersubjective,
interpersonal component in which God
reveals his love and asks ours in return. It
is at this point that there emerges the
function of church doctrines and of theological doctrines. For that function is to
explain and to defend the authenticity of
the church's witness to the revelation in
Christ Jesus.

As already explained, there was a
slight tincture of scientifically differentiated consciousness in the Greek councils.
In the medieval period there was under-
taken the systematic and collaborative task
of reconciling all that had been handed
down by the church from the past. A first
step was Abaelard's *Sic et non*, in which
some one hundred and fifty-eight propositions were both proved and disproved by
arguments from scripture, the Fathers, the
councils, and reason.[13] In a second step
there was developed the technique of the
quaestio: Abaelard's *non* became *videtur
quod non* and his *sic* became *sed contra*

est. To these were added a general response, in which principles of solution
were set forth, and specific responses in
which the principles were applied to the
conflicting evidence. A third step was the
composition of books of sentences that
collected and classified relevant passages
from scripture and subsequent tradition.
A fourth step were the commentaries on
the books of sentences in which the technique of the *quaestio* was applied to these
richer collections of materials. The fifth
step was to obtain a conceptual system
that would enable the theologian to give
coherent answers to all the questions he
raised; and this was obtained partly by
adopting and partly by adapting the
Aristotelian corpus.

Scholastic theology was a monumental
achievement. Its influence on the church
has been profound and enduring. Up to
Vatican II, which preferred a more biblical turn of speech, it has provided much
of the background whence proceeded
pontifical documents and conciliar decrees. Yet today by and large it is aban-

doned, and that abandonment leaves the documents and decrees that relied on it almost mute and ineffectual. Such is the contemporary crisis in Catholicism. It is important to indicate why it exists and how it can be overcome.

The Scholastic aim of reconciling all the documents of the Christian tradition had one grave defect; it was content with a logically and metaphysically satisfying reconciliation; it did not realize how much of the multiplicity in the inheritance constituted not a logical or metaphysical but basically a historical problem.

Secondly, the Aristotelian corpus, on which Scholasticism drew for the framework of its solutions suffers from a number of defects. The *Posterior Analytics* set forth an ideal of science in which the key element is the notion of necessity, of what cannot be otherwise. On this basis, science is said to be of the necessary, while opinion regards the contingent; similarly, wisdom is concerned with first principles, while prudence regards contingent human affairs. There follows the primacy of spec-

ulative intellect, and this is buttressed by
a verbalism that attributes to common
names the properties of scientific terms.
Finally, while man is acknowledged to be
a political animal, the historicity of the
meanings that inform human living is not
grasped, and much less is there understood the fact that historical meaning is to
be presented not by poets but by historians.

In contrast, modern mathematics is
fully aware that its axioms are not necessary truths but only freely chosen and no
more than probably consistent postulates.
The modern sciences ascertain, not what
must be so, but only what is in itself hypo-
thetical and so in need of verification.
First principles in philosophy are not verbal propositions but the *de facto* invariants
of human conscious intentionality. What
was named speculative intellect, now is
merely the operations of experiencing, understanding, and judging, performed under the guidance of the moral delibera-
tion, evaluation, decision, that selects a
method and sees to it that the method is

observed. The primacy now belongs to practical intellect and, perforce, philosophy ultimately becomes a philosophy of action. Finally, it is only on the basis of intentionality analysis that it is possible either to understand human historicity or to set forth the foundations and criticize the practice of contemporary hermeneutics and critical history.

The defects of Scholasticism, then, were the defects of its time. It could not inspect the methods of modern history and thereby learn the importance of history in theology. It could not inspect modern science and thereby correct the mistakes in Aristotle's conceptual system. But if we cannot blame the Scholastics for their shortcomings, we must undertake the task of remedying them. A theology is the product not only of a faith but also of a culture. It is cultural change that has made Scholasticism no longer relevant and demands the development of a new theological method and style, continuous indeed with the old, yet meeting all the genuine exigences both of the Christian religion and of up-to-date philosophy, science, and scholarship.

Until that need is met, pluralism will obtain. Undifferentiated consciousness will continue its ban on technical theology. Scientifically differentiated consciousness will ally itself with secularism. Religiously differentiated consciousness will know that the main issue is in the heart and not the head. Scholarly differentiated consciousness will continue to pour forth the fruits of its research in interpretations and histories. Philosophically differentiated consciousness will continue to twist and turn in its efforts to break loose from Kant's grasp. But the worthy successor to thirteenth century achievement will be the fruit of a fourfold differentiated consciousness, in which the workings of common sense, science, scholarship, intentionality analysis, and the life of prayer have been integrated.

6.   *Pluralism and Conversion*

Conversion involves a new understanding of oneself because, more fundamentally, it brings about a new self to be

understood. It is putting off the old man
and putting on the new. It is not just a
development but the beginning of a new
mode of developing. Hence, besides the
beginning, there is to be considered the
consequent development. This may be
great or average or small. It may be mar-
red by few or by many relapses. The relapses may have been corrected fully, or
they may still leave their traces in a bias
that may be grave or venial.

Conversion is three-dimensional. It is
intellectual inasmuch as it regards our
orientation to the intelligible and the true.
It is moral inasmuch as it regards our
orientation to the good. It is religious inasmuch as it regards our orientation to
God. The three dimensions are distinct, so
that conversion can occur in one dimension without occurring in the other two,
or in two dimensions without occurring in
the other one. At the same time, the three
dimensions are solidary. Conversion in
one leads to conversion in the other
dimensions, and relapse from one prepares
for relapse from the others.

By intellectual conversion a person frees himself from confusing the criteria of the world of immediacy with the criteria of the world mediated by meaning. By moral conversion he becomes motivated primarily not by satisfactions but by values. By religious conversion he comes to love God with his whole heart and his whole soul and all his mind and all his strength; and in consequence he loves his neighbor as himself.

The authentic Christian strives for the fulness of intellectual, moral, and religious conversion. Without intellectual conversion he tends to misapprehend not only the world mediated by meaning but also the word God has spoken within that world. Without moral conversion he tends to pursue not what truly is good but what only apparently is good. Without religious conversion he is radically desolate: in the world without hope and without God (Eph 2, 12).

While the importance of moral and religious conversion will readily be granted, hesitation will be felt by many when it

comes to intellectual conversion. They will
feel that it is a philosophic issue and that
it is not up to theologians to solve it. But
while these contentions are true, they are
not decisive. The issue is also existential
and methodical. Theologians have minds.
They have always used them. They may
use them properly and they may use them
improperly. Unless they find out the difference for themselves or learn about it
from someone else, they will be counten-
ancing a greater pluralism than can be
tolerated.

Indeed, in my opinion, intellectual
conversion is essentially simple. It occurs
spontaneously when one reaches the age
of reason, implicitly drops earlier criteria
of reality(are you awake?, do you see it?
is it heavy? etc.), and proceeds to operate
on the criteria of sufficient evidence or
sufficient reason. But this spontaneous
conversion is insecure. The use of the
earlier criteria can recur. It is particularly
likely to recur when one gets involved in
philosophic issues. For then the objectification of what is meant by sufficient evi-

dence or sufficient reason is exceedingly
complex, while the objectification of taking a good look is simplicity itself. So one
becomes a naive realist, or an empiricist,
or an idealist, or a pragmatist, or a pheno-
menologist, and so on.

Now, in any individual, conversion
can be present or absent; in the former
case it can be present in one dimension or
in two or in all three; it can be enriched
by development, or distorted by aberration, and the development and aberration
may be great or small. Such differences
give rise to another variety of pluralism.
Besides the pluralism implicit in the transition from classicist to modern culture,
besides the pluralism implicit in the co-
existence of undifferentiated and variously
differentiated consciousness, there is the
more radical pluralism that arises when all
are not authentically human and authentically Christian.

Unauthenticity may be open-eyed and
thorough-going, and then it heads for a
loss of faith. But the unconverted may
have no real apprehension of what it is to

be converted. Sociologically they are Catholics, but on a number of points they deviate from the norm. Moreover, they commonly will not have an appropriate language for expressing what they really are, and so they will use the language of the group with which they identify socially. There will result an inflation of language and so of doctrine. Terms that denote what one is not, will be stretched to denote what one is. Doctrines that are embarrassing will not be mentioned. Unacceptable conclusions will not be drawn. So unauthenticity can spread and become a tradition and, for those born into such a tradition, becoming authentic human beings will be a matter of purifying the tradition in which they were brought up.

Quite by itself the pluralism resulting from a lack of conversion can be perilous. But the dangers are multiplied many times when the lack of conversion combines with other modes of pluralism. The transition from classicist culture to modern historical-mindedness, if combined with lack of conversion, can amount to a water-

ing down of the faith. Undifferentiated
consciousness, combined with defective
conversion, will opt for the gospels and
drop the dogmas. Religiously differentiated consciousness without intellectual
conversion will deprecate insistence on
doctrines. Scholarly differentiated consciousness can unleash floods of informa-
tion in which origins are ever obscurer and
continuity hard to discern. The modern
philosophic differentiation of consciousness can prove a trap that confines one in
a subjectivism and a relativism.

7.   *Pluralism and Church Doctrines:*
      The First Vatican Council

On pluralism and church doctrines
there is an important pronouncement
made in the constitution, *Dei Filius,* pro-
mulgated by the first Vatican council. It
occurs in the last paragraph of the fourth
and final chapter of the decree (DS 3020)
and in the appended canon (DS 3043). It
is to the effect that there is ever to be retained that meaning of a dogma that was
once declared by the church, and that
there is to be no departure from it on the

pretext of some profounder understanding
(DS 3020). Moreover, this pronouncement at least historically has a reference to
pluralism. For earlier the Holy See had
condemned the thorough-going pluralism
of Anton Günther (DS 2828 ff.) and of
Jakob Frohschammer (DS 2850 ff.; cf.
2908 f.), and Cardinal Franzelin had pursued the matter further both in the *votum*
he presented to the preconciliar committee[14] and in his schema, *Contra errores ex
rationalismo derivatos,* presented for discussion in the early days of Vatican I.[15]

In true classicist style, however, the
fourth chapter is proceeding, not against
historical persons, but against errors. The
main thrust of chapter four, as appears
from the three appended canons (DS
3041-43), is against a rationalism that
considers mysteries non-existent, that pro-
poses to demonstrate the dogmas, that
defends scientific conclusions even though
opposed to church doctrines, that claims
the church to have no right to condemn
scientific views, and that grants science

the competence to reinterpret the church's
dogmas.

Against such rationalism the council
had distinguished (1) the natural light of
reason, (2) faith, (3) reason illumined by
faith, and (4) reason operating beyond its
proper limits.

Reason, then, or the natural light of
reason, has a range of objects within its
reach (DS 3015). It can know with certi-
tude the existence of God (DS 3004), and
it can know some though not all of the
truths revealed by God (DS 3005, 3015).
It must submit to divine revelation (DS
3008) and such submission is in harmony
with its nature (DS 3009). In no way does
the church prohibit human disciplines
from using their proper principles and
methods within their own fields (DS
3019).

Faith is a supernatural virtue by which
we believe to be true what God has revealed not because we apprehend the intrinsic truth of what has been revealed
but because of the authority of God who
reveals and can neither deceive nor be

deceived (DS 3008). By divine and catholic faith are to be believed all that is both revealed by God in scripture or tradition and, as well, has been proposed to be revealed either in a solemn pronouncement by the church or in the exercise of its ordinary and universal teaching office (DS 3011). Among the principal objects of faith, are the mysteries hidden in God which, were they not revealed, could not be known by us (DS 3015, cf. 3005).

Reason illumined by faith, when it inquires diligently, piously, soberly, reaches with God's help some extremely fruitful understanding of the mysteries both in virtue of the analogy of things it knows naturally and in virtue of the interconnection of the mysteries with one another and with man's last end. But it never becomes capable of grasping them after the fashion it grasps the truths that lie within its proper range. For the divine mysteries by their very nature so exceed created intellect that even when given by revelation and accepted by faith still by the veil of faith itself they remain as it were covered over by some sort of cloud (DS 3016). It would seem to be the understanding attained by reason illumined by faith that is praised in the quotation from Vincent of Lerins (DS 3020). For this understanding regards not some human invention, but the mysteries revealed by God and accepted on faith; and so from the nature of the case it will be "... in suo dumtaxat genere, in eodem scilicet dogmate, eodem sensu eademque sententia" (DS 3020).

Finally, there is reason that steps beyond its proper bounds to invade and disturb the realm of faith (DS 3019). For the doctrine of faith, which God has revealed, has not been proposed as some sort of philosophic discovery to be perfected by human talent. It is a divine deposit, given to the spouse of Christ, to be guarded faithfully and to be declared infallibly. Hence there is ever to be retained that meaning of the sacred dogmas that once was declared by holy mother church; and from that meaning there is to be no departure under the pretext of some profounder understanding (DS 3020).

In this passage a definite limit is placed on doctrinal pluralism. Similarly, in the corresponding canon, there is condemned anyone that says it is possible that eventually with the progress of science there may have to be given to the dogmas propounded by the church a meaning other than that which the church understood and understands (DS 3043).

First, then, there is affirmed a permanence of meaning: ". . . is sensus perpetuo est retinendus. . . . . . nec umquam ab eo recedendum . . . ." "in eodem scilicet dogmate, eodem sensu eademque sententia" (DS 3020). ". . . sensus tribuendus sit alius. . . ." (DS 3043).

Secondly, the permanent meaning is the meaning declared by the church (DS 3020), the meaning which the church understood and understands (DS 3043).

Thirdly, this permanent meaning is the meaning of dogmas (DS 3020, 3043). But from the context of the paragraph the meaning of dogmas has this permanence because it conveys the doctrine of faith, revealed by God, which was not proposed as a philosophic invention to be perfected by human talent.

Now God reveals both truths that lie within the range of human intelligence and divine mysteries, hidden in God, that could not be known unless they were revealed (DS 3015, 3005). It would seem that it is the mysteries that transcend the intelligence of the human mind (DS 3005) and by their very nature stand beyond created intellect (DS 3016) that are not mere philosophic inventions that human talent could perfect. On the other hand, truths that naturally are knowable would seem capable of being known more accurately with the progress of science (DS 3043).

It would seem, then, that dogmas refer to the church's declaration of revealed mysteries.

Fourthly, the meaning of the dogma is not apart from a verbal formulation, for it is a meaning declared by the church. However, the permanence attaches to the meaning and not to the formula. To retain the same formula and give it a new meaning is precisely what the third canon excludes (DS 3043).

Fifthly, it seems better to speak of the permanence of the meaning of dogmas rather than of the immutability of that meaning. For permanence is what is implied by *retinendus, non recedendum, non ... alius tribuendus.* Again, it is permanence rather than immutability that is meant when there is asserted a growth and advance in understanding, knowledge, wisdom with respect to the same dogma and the same meaning (DS 3020).

Finally, let us ask why the meaning of dogmas is permanent. There are two answers. The first assigns the *causa cognoscendi,* the reason why we know it to be permanent. The second assigns the *causa essendi,* the reason why it has to be permanent.

First, the *causa cognoscendi.* What God reveals, what the church infallibly declares, is true. What is true, is permanent. The meaning it had in its own context can never truthfully be denied.

Secondly, the *causa essendi*. The mysteries lie beyond the range of human intelligence (DS 3005), created intellect (DS 3016). They could not be known by us unless they were revealed (DS 3015). They are known by us, not because their intrinsic truth is grasped, but because of God's authority (DS 3008). Our understanding of them can increase when reason is illumined by faith; but it is an understanding of the revealed mystery—*in eodem dogmate* — and not of some human substitute for the mystery (DS 3016, 3020). It would be to disregard divine transcendence if one handed the mysteries over to philosophic or scientific reinterpretation.

Such, it seems to me, is the meaning of the pronouncement of the constitution, *Dei Filius,* with respect to the permanence of the meaning of the dogmas. But since the first Vatican council there have occurred further developments. While Anton Günther and Jakob Frohschammer were concerned with human historicity, the council was content simply to point out

where their views were unacceptable. It
did not attempt to integrate its contentions with what is true in the affirmation
of human historicity. To this topic we
must now attend.

8. *Pluralism and Church Doctrines*: *The Ongoing Context*

A statement has a meaning in a context. If one already knows the context, the
meaning of the statement is plain. If one
does not know the context, one discovers
it by asking questions. The answer to a
first question may suggest two further
questions. The answers to them suggest
still more. Gradually there is woven to-
gether an interlocking set of questions and
answers and, sooner or later, there is
reached a point where further questions
have less and less relevance to the matter
in hand. One could ask about this and that
and the other, but the answers would not
help one to understand better the meaning of the original statement. In brief there
is a limit to useful questioning, and when
that is reached the context is known.

Such is the prior context, the context within which the original statement was made and through which the original meaning of the statement is determined. But besides the prior context, there is also the subsequent context. For a statement may intend to settle one issue and to prescind from other issues. But settling the one does not burke the others. Usually it contributes to a clearer grasp of the others and a more urgent pressure for their solution. According to Athanasius the council of Nicea used a non-scriptural term in a confession of faith, not to set a precedent, but to meet an emergency. But the emergency lasted for thirty-five years, and, some twenty years after it had subsided, the first council of Constantinople felt it necessary to answer the question whether only the Son or also the Holy Spirit was consubstantial with the Father. Fifty years later at Ephesus, it was necessary to clarify Nicea by affirming that it was one and the same that was born of the Father and born of the Virgin Mary.

Twenty-one years later it was necessary to add that one and the same could be both eternal and temporal, both immortal and mortal, because he had two natures. Over two centuries later there was added the further clarification that the divine person that had two natures also had two operations and two wills. Within this matrix there arose a series of questions about Christ as man. Could he sin? Did he feel concupiscence? Was he in any way ignorant? Did he have sanctifying grace? To what extent? Did he have immediate knowledge of God? Did he know everything pertaining to his mission? Such is the Christological context that did not exist prior to Nicea but, bit by bit, came into existence subsequently to Nicea. It does not state what was intended at Nicea. It does state what resulted from Nicea and what became in fact the context within which Nicea was to be understood.

As one may distinguish prior and subsequent ages in an ongoing context, so one ongoing context may be related to another.

Of these relations the commonest are derivation and interaction. The Christological context, that was built up by answering questions that stemmed from the decision at Nicea, was itself derived from the earlier tradition expressed in the New Testament, by the apostolic Fathers, by orthodox Judaic Christianity, by the Christian apologists, and by the later antenicene Fathers. Again, out of the whole of earlier Christian thought there was derived the ongoing context of medieval theology, and this ongoing context interacted with subsequently developed church doctrines, as is clear from the dependence of theologians on church authority and, inversely, from Scholastic influence on pontifical and conciliar statements up to the second Vatican council.

Now such ongoing contexts are subject to many influences. They are distorted by the totally or partly unconverted that usually are unaware of the imperfections of their outlook. They are divided by the presence of people with undifferentiated or differently differentiated consciousness.

They are separated because members of
different cultures construct different contexts by finding different questions relevant and different answers intelligible.

Such differences give rise to a pluralism, and the pluralism gives rise to incom-
prehension and exasperation. The unconverted cannot understand the converted,
and the partly converted cannot understand the totally converted. Inversely, because they are misunderstood, the converted are exasperated by the unconverted. Again, undifferentiated consciousness does not understand differentiated
consciousness, and partially differentiated
consciousness does not understand a fourfold differentiated consciousness. Inversely, because it is met with incomprehen-
sion more adequately differentiated consciousness is exasperated by less adequately differentiated consciousness. Finally,
our historically minded contemporaries
have no difficulty understanding the ghettos in which a classicist mentality still
reigns, but the people in the classicist
ghettos not only have no experience of

serious historical investigation but also are quite unaware of the historicity of their own assumptions.

There exists, then, a stubborn fact of pluralism. It is grounded in cultural difference, in greater or less differentiation of consciousness, and in the presence and absence of religious, moral, and intellectual conversion. How such pluralism is to be met within the unity of faith, is a question yet to be considered. But first we must attempt to indicate how to reconcile the permanence with the historicity of the dogmas.

9. *The Permanence and the Historicity of Dogma.*

The meaning of the dogmas is permanent because that meaning is not a datum but a truth, and that truth is not human but divine. The data of sense are merely given. As merely given, they are not yet understood, and much less is there any understanding verified as probably true. Even when understood and when the understanding is probably verified, there ever remains the possibility of the dis-

covery of still further relevant data that
may compel a revision of earlier views.
But the dogmas are not data but truths,
and the truths proceed, not from human
understanding and verification, but from
God's understanding of himself in his transcendence. There is no possibility of man
in this life improving on God's revelation
of the mysteries hidden in God, and so the
meaning of the dogmas, because it is true,
is permanent and, because it is concerned
with the divine mysteries, it is not subject
to human revision.

However, meaning can be grasped only
by grasping its context. The meaning of
a dogma is the meaning of a declaration
made by the church at a particular place
and time and within the context of that
occasion. Only through the historical study
of that occasion and the exegetical study
of that declaration can one arrive at the
proper meaning of the dogma.

Now this historicity of dogma has been
obscured by the massive continuity that
the church has been able to build up and
maintain. The dogmas clustered into a

single ongoing context. That context merged into a static, classicist culture to influence it profoundly. There was developed a theoretical theology that integrated both the dogmas and the theology with a philosophic view of the cosmos. The philosophic view was derived from one main source and its unity was further strengthened by the dogmas. Finally, the scholarly differentiation of consciousness was rarely attained so that cultural and other differences tended to be overlooked.

Today however classicist culture has yielded place to modern culture with its dynamism and its worldwide pluralism. The sciences seek to occupy the whole realm of theory, and philosophy is driven to migrate to the realm of interiority, or of religion, or of art, or of the undifferentiated consciousness of some brand of common sense. Such philosophic pluralism is radical. Further, scholars have become a large, collaborative, methodical group with an enormous output that only specialists can follow. Theologians can be tempted to desert theology for scholarship.

Theologians and scholars can regard recourse to philosophy as foolhardy. Religiously differentiated consciousness can remain assured that religion is a matter not for the head but for the heart.

Such by and large is the contemporary situation. For many, to whom the meaning of the word, truth, is obscure, it is not enough to say that the dogmas are permanent because they are true. They want to to know whether the dogmas are permanently relevant.

10. *Pluralism and The Unity of Faith*

There are three sources of pluralism. First, linguistic, social, and cultural differences give rise to different brands of common sense. Secondly, consciousness may be undifferentiated or it may differentiate to deal effectively with such realms as those of common sense, transcendence, theory, scholarship, interiority. Such differentiations may be single or they may combine so that, mathematically, there are sixteen different ways (thirty-two if the realm of the aesthetic is added) in which consciousness may be structured and so

envisage its world. Thirdly, in any individual at any time there may be the mere
beginnings, or greater or less progress, or
the high development of intellectual, of
moral, and of religious conversion. Finally,
the foregoing sets of differences are cumulative. One is born in a given linguistic,
social, and cultural milieu. One's consciousness remains undifferentiated or it
differentiates in any of a number of manners. One may fail to attain any type of
conversion; one may attain conversion in
one or two or all three manners; and the
conversion attained may be followed up
by greater or less development.

Pluralism is not something new. But in
the past a number of devices served either
to eliminate it or to cover over its existence. Culture was conceived normatively.
What is normative also is universal, if not
de facto then at least *de iure*. Though there
did exist the simple faithful, the people,
the natives, the barbarians, still career was
open to talent. One entered upon it by dili-
gent study of the ancient Latin and Greek
authors. One pursued it by learning Scho-

lastic philosophy and theology and canon
law. One exercised it by one's fluent teaching or conduct of affairs in the Latin
tongue. It was quite a system in its day,
but now its day is over. We have to call
on other resources.

First, then, the root and ground of unity
is being in love with God, the fact that
God's love has flooded our hearts through
the Holy Spirit he has given us (Rom 5,
5). The acceptance of that gift constitutes
religious conversion and leads to moral and
to intellectual conversion.

Secondly, religious conversion, if it is
Christian, is not just a state of mind and
heart. Essential to it is an intersubjective,
interpersonal component. Besides the gift
of the Spirit within, there is the outward
encounter with Christian witness. That
witness recalls the fact that of old in many
ways God has spoken to us through the
prophets but in this latest age through his
Son (Heb 1, 1.2).

Thirdly, the function of church doctrines lies within the function of witness.
For the witness is to the mysteries revealed

by God and, for Catholics, infallibly declared by the church. Their meaning is beyond the vicissitudes of human historical process. But the contexts, within which such meaning is grasped and expressed, vary both with cultural differences and with the measure in which consciousness is differentiated.

Such variation is familiar to us from the past. According to Vatican II, revelation occurred not through words alone but through deeds and words. The apostolic preaching was addressed not only to Jews in the thought-forms of *Spätjudentum* but also to Greeks in their language and idiom. The New Testament writings spoke more to the heart than the head, but the Christological councils aimed solely at formulating truth to guide one's mind and lips. When Scholastic theology recast Christian belief into a mould derived from Aristotle, it was deserting neither divine revelation nor scripture nor the councils. And if modern theologians were to transpose medieval theory into terms derived from modern interiority and its real correlatives, they

would do for our age what the Scholastics
did for theirs.

There has existed, then, a notable pluralism of expression. Currently in the
church there is quietly disappearing the
old classicist insistence on worldwide uni-
formity, and there is emerging a pluralism
of the manners in which Christian meaning and Christian values are communicated. To preach the gospel to all nations
is to preach it to every class in every culture in the manner that accords with the
assimilative powers of that class and culture.

For the most part such preaching will
be to undifferentiated consciousness, and
so it will have to be as multiform as are
the diverse brands of common sense gen-
erated by the many languages, social
forms, and cultural meanings and values
of mankind. In each case the preacher will
have to know the brand of common sense
to which he speaks, and he will have ever
to keep in mind the fact that in undifferentiated consciousness coming to know
does not occur apart from acting.

But if the faith is to be nourished in those whose consciousness is undifferentiated, those with differentiated consciousness are not to be neglected. Now just as the only way to understand another's brand of common sense is to come to understand the way he or she would understand, speak, act in any of the series of situations that commonly arise, so too the only way to understand another's differentiation of consciousness is to bring about that differentiation in oneself.

Now each differentiation of consciousness involves a certain remodelling of common sense. Initially common sense assumes its own omnicompetence because it just cannot know better. But as successive differentiations of consciousness occur, more and more realms are entered in the appropriate fashion and so are removed from the competence of common sense. Clarity and adequacy increase by bounds. One's initial common sense is purged of its simplifications, its metaphors, its myths, its mystifications. With the attainment of full differentiation, common sense is confined entirely to its proper field of the immediate, the particular, the concrete.

However, there are many routes to full attainment and many varieties of partial attainment. Preaching the gospel to all means preaching it in the manner appropriate to each of the varieties of partial attainment and, no less, to full attainment. It was to meet the exigences proper to the beginnings of theoretically differentiated consciousness that Clement of Alexandria denied that the anthropomorphisms of scripture were to be interpreted literally.[16] It was to meet the exigences proper to the full theoretical differentiation of consciousness that medieval Scholasticism sought a coherent account of all the truths of faith and reason. It was to meet the exigences of a scholarly differentiation of consciousness that the second Vatican council decreed that the interpreter of scripture had to determine the meaning intended by the biblical writer and accordingly had to do so by understanding the literary conventions and cultural conditions of his place and time.[17]

The church, then, following the example of St. Paul, becomes all things to all men (I Cor. 9, 22). It communicates what God has revealed both in the manner appropriate to the various differentiations of consciousness and, above all, in the manner appropriate to each of the almost endless brands of common sense, especially of undifferentiated consciousness. But these many modes of speech constitute no more than a pluralism of communications, for all can be *in eodem dumtaxat genere, in eodem scilicet dogmate, eodem sensu eademque sententia.*

Still, becoming all to all, even though it involves no more than a pluralism of communications, none the less is not without its difficulties. On the one hand, it demands a many-sided development in those that teach and preach. On the other hand, every achievement is apt to be challenged by those that fail to achieve. Those that are not scholars can urge that attending to the literary genre of biblical writings is just a fraudulent device for rejecting the plain meaning of scripture. While theorists

insist that one must feel compunction before attempting to define it, non-theorists
suggest the contrary by asserting that it is
better to feel compunction than to define
it. Those whose undifferentiated consciousness is unmitigated by any tincture
of theory will not grasp the meaning of
dogmas such as that of Nicea and they
may leap gayly to the conclusion that what
has no meaning for them is just meaning-
less.

Such difficulties suggest such rules as
the following. First, because the gospel is
to be preached to all, there must be sought
the modes of representation and expression appropriate to communicating revealed truth both to every brand of common sense and to every differentiation of
consciousness. Secondly, no one simply because of his faith is obliged to attain one
or more differentiations of consciousness.
Thirdly, no one simply because of his faith
is obliged to refrain from attaining an ever
more differentiated consciousness. Fourthly, anyone may strive to express his faith

in the manner appropriate to his differentiation of consciousness. Fifthly, no one
should pass judgment on matters he does
not understand, and the statements of a
more differentiated consciousness are not
going to be understood by persons with a
less or a differently differentiated consciousness.

Finally, there is the type of pluralism
that results from the presence or absence
of intellectual, of moral, or of religious
conversion. It is this type of pluralism
that is perilous to unity in the faith especially when a lack of conversion exists in
those that govern the church or teach in
the church. Moreover, the dangers are
multiplied when, as at present, there is
going forward in the church a movement
out of classicist culture and into modern
culture, when persons with differentiated
consciousness not only do not understand
one another but so extol either advanced
prayer, or theory, or scholarship, or interiority, as to exclude development and set
aside achievement in the other three.

11. *The Permanence of Dogma and Demythologization*

Cosmogonies, myths, sagas, legends, apocalypses arise at a time when distinct functions of meaning are not distinguished. Meaning is not only communicative. It is a constitutive element in human living, knowing, and doing. But this constitutive function is overextended when it is employed to constitute not only man's being in the world but also the world man is in.

To demythologize is to confine constitutive meaning within its proper bounds. This is a very long task and so different stages in the process have to be distinguished.[18]

The earliest stage is the reinterpretation of myth. Thought is still prephilosophic and prescientific, and so there still occur the types of expression that philosophy and science will eliminate. None the less, older myth is being purified. In the Old Testament there is no primeval battle of gods, no divine generation of kings or chosen peoples, no cult of the stars or of sexuality, no sacralization of the fruitful-ness of nature. God's action is his action in a history of salvation, and the account of creation in Genesis is the opening of the story. Similarly, in the New Testament the faith of the community is directed towards God's saving acts in an earthly history. Elements of apocalyptic and gnostic mythology are employed only to facilitate the expression of the faith and, when they fail to do so, they are rigorously excluded.[19]

A second stage is philosophic. It begins, perhaps, with Xenophanes who noticed that the gods of the Ethiopians look like Ethiopians while the gods of the Thracians look like Thracians. He also contended that if lions and horses and oxen had hands and could do such works as men do, then the gods of the lions would resemble lions, the gods of the horses would resemble horses, and the gods of the oxen would resemble oxen. The point was picked up by Clement of Alexandria who taught that the anthropomorphisms of the bible were not to be taken literally and, thereby, started the century-long ef-

forts of Christians to conceive God on the
analogy of spirit rather than of matter.[20]

The third stage is theological. If God
is to be conceived on the analogy of spirit,
then in God there can be Father and Son
only if there can be some sort of spiritual
generation. So Origen conceived the Son
to proceed from the Father as an act of
will from the mind, Augustine found his
analogy in the origin of inner word from
true knowledge, while Aquinas showed
how the origin of concept from understanding could be named a generation.[21]
In similar fashion systematic theologians
down the ages have sought analogies that
yielded some fruitful understanding of the
mysteries.

A fourth stage is scientific. Copernicus
gave the first thrust towards a transformation of man's image of the universe, Darwin did as much for a transformation of
man's notion of the origin of his body,
Freud invaded the secrets of his soul. While
neither Copernicus nor Darwin nor Freud
have uttered the last word in their respec-

tive fields, still we no longer argue from
the bible against them.

A fifth stage is scholarly. Hermeneutics
and critical history have disrupted the
classicist dream of a single standardized
culture with the consequence of a standardized man. There has been discovered
human historicity—the fact that, while abstract concepts are immutable in virtue of
their abstractness, none the less human
understanding keeps developing to express
itself in ever different images and slogans
and to replace earlier by later abstractions.

A sixth stage is post-Scholastic theology. It has to comprehend the previous
five stages. It has to discover the invariants of human development. It has to take
its stand both on inner religious experience and on the historicity of personal development within the Christian community.

So understood, demythologization is
simply the ongoing growth and advance
of understanding, knowledge, and wisdom,
desired by the first Vatican council (DS
3020). It can eliminate misconceptions of

what God did reveal. But it is powerless
against anything that God really did reveal
and the church infallibly has declared.

Finally, let me note that demythologization in the foregoing sense is quite different from Rudolf Bultmann's *Entmyth-
ologisierung*. The latter's views arise in a
quite peculiar context. Modern scholarship derives from the German Historical
School of the early nineteenth century.
While it expressed a reaction against
Hegel's apriorist views on the meaning of
history, it was far from resembling strict
empirical science in which there are added
to the data only an understanding that
arises from the data. As Wilhelm Dilthey
discovered, the Historical School was full
of ideas derived from the Enlightenment
and even from Hegel.[22] What eliminated
from historical scholarship such alien influences, was simply a positivist empiri-
cism that ruled out other presuppositions
and postulated that human history be a
closed field of causally interconnected
events.[23] Such a view of history has been
rejected by such historians as Carl Becker

in the United States, R. G. Collingwood in England, H. I. Marrou in France. But the outstanding theological reaction was effected by Karl Barth and Rudolf Bultmann. They took their stand on moral and religious conversion. But they did not advert to the fact that besides moral and religious conversion there also is intellectual conversion. Accordingly, they were incapable of effecting any serious criticism of the philosophic presuppositions of the historicism in vogue at the beginning of this century. Very summarily, Barth was content with a fideist affirmation of Christian truth. Bultmann did "scientific" work on the New Testament, while his morally and religiously converted being assented to the locally preached kerygma of the fact of God's self-revelation in Christ Jesus.

1. This distinction was drawn by Pope John XXIII in his opening address at Vatican II. See AAS 54 (1962), 792 lines 8 ff.

2. See for example Jean Daniélou *Théologie du judéo-christianisme,* Tournai & Paris (Desclée) 1959); E. T., London (Darton, Longman & Todd) 1964. *Les symboles Chrétiens primitifs,* Paris (du Seuil) 1961; E. T., London (Burns & Oates) and Baltimore (Helicon) 1964. *Études d'exégèse judéo-chrétienne,* Paris (Beauchesne) 1966.

3. For a sketch see the essay, "Cognitional Structure," in *Collection,* Papers by B. Lonergan edited by F. E. Crowe, New York (Herder & Herder) and London (Darton, Longman & Todd) 1967, pp. 221-239.

4. On the relativist contention that context is infinite, see B. Lonergan, *Insight,* London (Longmans) and New York (Philosophical Library) 1957, ⁹1970, pp. 342 ff.

5. On the Kantian notion of object, briefly, B. Lonergan, *Collection,* p. 208; at length, J. Colette *et al., Procès de l'objectivité de Dieu,* Paris (du Cerf) 1969.

6. See William Johnston, *The Mysticism of the Cloud of Unknowing,* New York, Rome, Tournai, Paris (Desclée) 1967; also *The Still Point,* New York (Fordham) 1970, pp. 27 ff. Karl Rahner, *The Dynamic Element in the Church,* Montreal (Palm) and Freiburg (Herder) 1964, pp. 129 ff.

7. The five are: scientific and scholarly; scientific and philosophic; religious and scholarly; religious and philosophic; scholarly and philosophic.

8.   The four are scientific, religious, and scholarly; scientific, religious, and philosophic; scientific, scholarly, and philosophic; religious, scholarly and philosophic.

9.   Athanasius, *Oratio III c. Arianos*, 4, *MG* 26, 329 A.

10.   DS 301 f.

11.   See Johnston or Rahner cited above, note 6.

12.   On the transition from Vatican I to the contemporary context on natural knowledge of God, see my paper: "Natural Knowledge of God," *Proceedings, Catholic Theological Society of America*, 23 (1968), 54-69.

13.   *ML* 178, 1339 ff.

14.   The *votum* has been published in an appendix to the work of Herman J. Pottmeyer, *Der Glaube vor dem Anspruch der Wissenschaft*, Freiburg (Herder) 1968, see especially Anhang, pp. 50*, 51*, 54*, 55*. The author, to whom we are indebted, has some twenty-five pages on the passage with which we are concerned.

15.   See chapters V, VI, XI, XII, and XIV of the schema, Mansi 50, 62-69 and the abundant annotations, Mansi 50, 83 ff.

16.   Clemens Alex., *Strom.* V, 11; 68, 3; *MG* 9, 103 B; Stählin II, 371, 18 ff.; also V, 11; 71, 4; *MG* 110A; Stählin II, 374, 15.

17.   *Const. dogm. de Revelatione* III, 12.

18.   One instance of the process has been convincingly described by Bruno Snell, *The Discovery of the Mind*, New York (Harper) 1960. This contains a chapter not in the original: *Die Entdeckung des Geistes*, Hamburg (Claassen und Goverts) 1948.

19. I am summarizing Kurt Frör, *Biblische Hermeneutik*, München (Kaiser) 1964, pp. 71 f.
20. See note 16 for reference to Clement.
21. Origen, *De princ.*, 1, 2, 6; Koetschau 35, 40 Augustine, *De trin.*, XV, 12 xii, 22; *ML* 42, 1075. Aquinas, *Sum. theol.*, 1, q. 27, a. 2.
22. See H. G. Gadamer, *Wahrheit und Methode*, Tübingen (Mohr) 1960, ²1965, pp. 185 f.
23. Frör, *op. cit.*, pp. 28 f.

The Pere Marquette Theology Lectures

1969: "The Authority for Authority,"
by Quentin Quesnell
Professor of Theology at
Marquette University

1970: "Mystery and Truth,"
by John Macquarrie
Professor of Theology at
Union Theological Seminary, New York

1971: "Doctrinal Pluralism,"
by Bernard Lonergan, S.J.
Professor of Theology at
Regis College, Ontario

1972: "Infallibility,"
by George A. Lindbeck
Professor of Theology at
Yale University

1973: "Ambiguity in Moral Choice,"
by Richard A. McCormick, S.J.
Professor of Moral Theology at
Bellarmine School of Theology

1974: "Church Membership as a Catholic
and Ecumenical Problem,"
by Avery Dulles, S.J.
Professor of Theology at
Woodstock College

1975: "The Contributions of Theology to
Medical Ethics,"
by James Gustafson
University Professor of Theological Ethics at
University of Chicago

1976: "Religious Values in an Age of Violence,"
by Rabbi Marc Tanenbaum
Director of National Interreligious Affairs
American Jewish Committee, New York City

1977: "Truth Beyond Relativism: Karl Mannheim's
Sociology of Knowledge,"
by Gregory Baum
Professor of Theology and Religious Studies at
St. Michael's College

Copies of this lecture and the others in the series are obtainable from:

Marquette University Press
Marquette University
Milwaukee, Wisconsin 53233
USA